2 COPIES

2

CH00735267

Where

PLEASE RETURN

CARL MIER LIBRARY

BELROW HOUSE.

OLFIELD LANE. ALDENHAM

WATFORD HERTS

Where Are You?

Coming to Terms
with the Death of my Child

Karin von Schilling

Anthroposophic Press
Hudson, New York

Published by Anthroposophic Press, Inc., Bell's Pond,
Star Route, Hudson, New York, 12534.

© 1988 by Karin von Schilling

Library of Congress Cataloging-in-Publication Data

Von Schilling, Karin.
    Where are you? : coming to terms with the death of
my child /Karin von Schilling.
    p. cm.
    Bibliography: p.
    ISBN 0-88010-268-3
    1. Bereavement—Religious   aspects—Anthroposo-
phy. 2. Anthroposophy. 3. Children—Death—Psycho-
logical aspects. 4. Consolation. 5. Von Schilling, Karin.
BP596.B47V66   1988
299'.935—dc19   88-24205
                                                            CIP

All rights reserved. No part of this book may be repro-
duced in any form without the written permission of the
publisher except for brief quotations embodied in criti-
cal reviews and articles.

Printed in the United States of America

Contents

PLEASE RETURN TO
CARL MIER LIBRARY
OELROW HOUSE
RIFFIELD LANE, ALDENHAM
WATFORD HERTS

Preface

On March 9, 1979 at 3:30 P.M., my thirteen-year-old daughter, my only child, died instantly in a head-on car crash.

Saskia and three other children were being driven home from school by a young mother. The usual driver for this day's lift-club had had trouble with his car and repairs were necessary.

The young mother, Mrs. Rudert, who had left her own three-year-old child at home—he had not wanted to come for the drive—took an unusual route, the quickest in her estimation. It was a small, winding road through a suburb, and was not used much any longer since a highway had been built alongside. It was considered dangerous and passing was illegal. We had also occasionally used the route.

Mrs. Rudert drove a small Volkswagen Beetle. The children were probably eager to get home to play, swim, or, in Saskia's case, to ride her pony. As the little car rounded a corner, a large Mercedes passed an oncoming truck. The Beetle was crushed and thrown to the other side of the road.

There were no survivors from the wreckage of the Beetle to describe what had happened. The young mother and two of the children, Anton and Saskia, were killed instantly. Two boys, Marcus and Martin, aged eleven and thirteen, were taken by ambulance to the General Hospital in Johannesburg, some twenty-five kilometers away. Both were unconscious. Marcus, the

vii

eleven year old, died three days later; he never regained consciousness.

Martin spent two months in a deep coma. Gradually he returned to consciousness. Continuous, selfless care was administered to him by many doctors and nurses, and prayers and loving thoughts called him back to life. Gradually he regained the use of his body, his speech, and, finally, his ability to recognize and to think; however, he faced the future as a handicapped person. He would often say, especially in the first years after the accident, "Why didn't I go with the others? Why did I have to stay on?" But as the years went by, he came to terms with his destiny in a very wonderful way, which I deeply admire.

Together with the parents of the other children, I had been called by the police. We had already been a little anxious; it was later than usual and our children were not home yet. The phone rang at 4:00 P.M. and a voice said, "There has been an accident. Please come to the General Hospital." I was stunned. I didn't know what to say. The person on the other end of the line realized the severity of the situation and added: "Take someone with you; it was a bad one."

How often had I read a short notice in a newspaper: "Child Killed in Accident"? Now, the unthinkable had happened to me!

A friend drove me into the city, a half hour's drive away. My heart pleaded incessantly, "Please hang on, dear love! I am coming! It will be alright!" At the emergency entrance of the hospital, life proceeded as usual. The other parents had also arrived. We all asked for our children. There was a long, agonizing wait. Finally, a nurse told us that two boys were being cared for in the adjacent rooms. The others were not at the hospital. My friend said simply, "She has gone."

In that very moment, my life was irreversibly changed. A desperate search, a silent cry, began, which was to last for years.

Very few of my many good friends, from near or far, were able to give me any real help. Lots of love and sympathy, and many kind thoughts, reached me, but they helped little. No one seemed able to really grasp or *feel* what had happened. The finality was overwhelming.

It is this awareness that urges me to write this book. I want to reach out to those who have had to suffer and endure a similar experience.

There is nothing spectacular to report, no visions or extraordinary experiences. I consciously stayed away from any spiritualistic approach. I had only the help of my living relationship to anthroposophy, or in other words, the awareness of the spiritual in the world and in people. I had learned to live with Rudolf Steiner's thoughts and words. His many published lectures and books had accompanied me over the years before the accident. They comforted and strengthened me at the time of this crucial blow of destiny, and during the years that followed.

It is in deep gratitude to Rudolf Steiner, with whose help I survived inwardly, that I want to write down for others something of what I learned. I want to share the fruits of these years, months, weeks, and days of anguish, and yet of hope.

1

The First Days

From the moment my friend told me, "She is gone," I entered a way of existence that I can only call shock consciousness. I did not scream or break down. Life continued. It was as if I looked down onto myself from outside my body. I saw myself move and act reasonably, rationally. I was principal of a Camphill therapeutic community for handicapped children and adolescents. It was my task to call the members of the staff together, to tell them what had happened and to arrange for a gathering in the evening: to read a prayer together, and to find the words that would send Saskia our love on this first night.

The accident had happened on a Friday afternoon. Because the weekend was ahead, the bodies of our children had been taken from the hospital to the mortuary. Nothing happened over Saturday and Sunday. Only on Monday could the official identification take place, and arrangements be made for burial or cremation. Those two days and nights passed so slowly!

Although Saskia and I had lived in a larger community, we had in effect been alone. There were no other children, and no husband to demand or divert my attention. Three friends had come to be at my side. Despite my outwardly steady behavior, my own reality was shattered. I stood at the edge of an abyss. The material, physical world seemed rather like a wall of rigid boards that had been put up to bar me from reaching beyond.

The co-workers, my friends, and I, met each of the three evenings preceding the funeral. Once was to speak about Saskia and her life. We included all our older pupils, to whom she had become a friend and with whom she had willingly shared her life. Another evening we met to learn some songs Saskia had known so well, and which we wanted to sing at her funeral. It would be good to sing the songs she had loved as a final farewell. We hoped she would hear us.

Although I managed to conduct these affairs, I experienced a total vacuum. For me space and time, in the usual sense, had stood still. This sensation continued for many months and years, long after I had taken up my active working life again.

Although Saskia's body lay elsewhere, in a cold, dreadful, and impersonal mortuary, some of us wanted to accompany her soul and wake with her for the first three nights. We arranged watches during these nights, taking turns to sit quietly with a few lit candles and a photograph, sending her warmth and loving thoughts.

The first three days and nights after death are of special importance. The soul of the one who has left her body has, during these days and nights, a vivid vision of her total life on earth. Her life is seen from the end to the beginning, like a huge panorama, or a script read in reverse order. It includes all the memories, all the people, all the places, and all the events that have been inscribed upon that soul.

These first three days and nights are kept sacred in many churches; funerals take place only after they have passed. In previous ages, people understood why. They knew that it takes these three days for the soul to loosen itself from the body before leaving it and expanding into the cosmos.

Saskia had gone! But where, where had she gone?

I had to choose. There was a need to decide: Should Saskia be cremated or buried?

Rudolf Steiner (1861–1925), the initiator of the anthroposophical movement, advised that for the person who has died it does not matter. It is for the ones who live on that the mode of funeral is meaningful and makes all the difference.

Saskia was a child; she had not yet even reached puberty. She was well built, healthy, and suntanned. She had loved being outdoors, spending her free time at the swimming pool or on her horse. She had brown eyes and short brown hair, always windblown. A true tomboy, she loved to walk barefoot, wearing T-shirts and shorts in preference to dresses. The very first signs of girlhood had made their tender appearance only recently; moments of gentleness, and an occasional flower in her hair, shyly worn, were small signs of acceptance of her growing femininity.

Her sudden death, tearing her out of life so utterly unprepared, must have been a severe shock to her, I reasoned. I felt that being now confined to the coldness of the mortuary, she could not bear to be given over to the other extreme: the fiery heat of cremation. But above all, I did not want to part with her body again; I wanted her buried at Cresset, the residential center that was our home. I prayed for permission for this, though it was most unlikely that it would be granted. It was my desire to lay her body under a large oak tree in a place she had loved, and one she had helped to develop.

It was utter grace: permission was given for the burial in home ground.

On Monday evening her body was brought to the Cresset Hall. I experienced a strange joy amidst all the despair. At last Saskia, or rather her body, had come back to me. Her face was still and clear. My heart inaudibly spoke to her: They have hurt you terribly, my dearest love!

The burial was to take place on Tuesday. Some of us watched at the side of her coffin for the last night in our Hall, all night. There were lots of flowers, candles, tokens of love, and a feeling of awareness from all over the world, for many had known Saskia.

But as the hours of the night advanced, I finally realized: She is gone. The words of the angel to the women who came to Christ's sepulcher came to my mind: "He whom ye seek, He is not here."[1] It was not blasphemy to think of this parallel. While we sat with the open coffin before us, it was a thread to cling to, for the experience could not be grasped by ordinary thoughts. It was fathomless.

In the morning, my soul was as if burnt out. My only intention was to try to be very quiet, so that Saskia would be able to hear through me the words of the funeral service. There were moments when a great inner calm filled me; I felt that it was Saskia herself helping me.

They buried her body in a deep grave, cut into the very hard, stone-like earth by some of my young co-workers. An abundance of flowers helped to soften the severity of the act. We sang her favorite songs, while classmates each dropped a rose onto the coffin, until the grave was filled up and covered with flowers. Then it was over; everyone left.

My long, long journey in search of Saskia now began.

I realized I was carried by a strong stream of life that was beyond human capacity. The sun rose as ever. The noises, be it the people in the shops, or the songs of birds, simply continued.

My body also continued to live and to function. A body that lived, as hers had lived only a short while ago, both borne through life by the same powerful force, yet hers had been torn away, while mine continued. The powerful rhythm of life went on, even if I remained motionless, even if time had stopped for me. Was this a dream, or was it a nightmare? I so hoped to wake up and find that this hadn't happened. We seem to go through life so unaware. I wanted to wake up! But how?

I felt physically exhausted and faint. And then, finally, the relief of tears. Animals cannot cry, however much pain they may experience. In the Apocalypse of St. John we read of the heavenly Jerusalem, where there will be eternal day and "God will wipe away all tears."

Tears, what a blessing they are! Every journey to the inner abyss, the experience of helplessness, of separation, of fathomless despair, ended in tears.

Maybe one day every unshed tear will turn into a pearl of inner clarity and strength; I had read this in the teachings of a great, wise woman in her book, *Light on the Path*.[2] But for me, tears saved me again and again from becoming confused, paralyzed, even insane, as to my own reality or any reality at all.

However, I thought, tears alone will not help. What can I do for Saskia?

2

The Search

Now the long, lonely road began. People more often than not preferred to avoid speaking of my daughter's death. No doubt they felt sorry, but did not know what to say; many tended literally to look the other way.

And yet, there was nothing I needed more than to talk about Saskia. To call her back to life, as the saying goes, was what I wanted. To reassure myself that she was real and had been alive not so long ago!

This I want to say to anyone who meets someone suddenly bereft of a loved one: join in the loving recollection of the one gone. Say something appreciative of her; it really helps.

Is it perhaps not only for oneself that this recalling is needed? It is now very clear to me that it is also a need for the one who has left, especially if the death was sudden and unexpected. We know this from Rudolf Steiner, and his descriptions have been confirmed more recently by many who were called back again, having already touched upon the threshold of death.[1]

Thus, we know that the soul of a departed person first experiences life in an enormous imaginative tableau, seeing its whole course; this takes place during the first three days and nights. After that, the visual panorama dissolves into the world-ether, and the soul now begins its backward walk through life—from the last day to the beginning. This is said to take about one-third of the person's lifetime, in earthly time-reckoning. Thus, if a person has reached the age of twenty-four years, it would take eight years to retrace the experiences of his or her life on earth.

In the case of children, Rudolf Steiner tells us that they, having accumulated very little experience and no guilt, pass through this time of atonement for one's failures and weaknesses, one's kamaloka, much faster, and in fact return to the golden sphere of our heavenly origin without much delay.

In the weeks of anguish, one reaches out to *any* description that can help to reassure one of the continuing existence of a beloved child. For brief moments one may find support in reading descriptions others have given: books that tell of a life hereafter; messages given, maybe even by way of a medium. I grasped desperately at any straw. It was as if I needed to be reassured again and again, to avoid literally sinking into a bottomless abyss of unreality.

Books I found most helpful, which I discovered only after searching for help, were recent descriptions of survivors of road accidents, such as *Mike*, or *Testimony of Light*[2] by Helen Greave, or *Return from Tomorrow*[3] by George Ritchie, and *Though You Die*[4] by Stanley Drake. They gave varying descriptions that I did not find easy to grasp or understand, but at least I could enter into a dialogue with them.

I discovered that talking with people about what had happened, and receiving advice, had its limits. I felt far too vulnerable. Words, just words, did not help.

Does anyone really understand, can they know what it feels like? Perhaps only those who have experienced a similar loss can identify with a bereaved parent. Most other people become strangers; one is alone. But reading by oneself is different. One can dwell on a sentence, ponder on or close the book and let it rest.

The most support I derived, however, was from reading lectures by Rudolf Steiner. In them I found clear, acceptable convictions based on the knowledge and supersensible experience of the soul's continued life after laying down its body; facts that were thinkable. They brought some order into my confused feelings.

Rudolf Steiner describes in detail the journey through different areas of experience as well as planetary spheres on the way to the ultimate expansion into the infinite. His descriptions have nothing sensational; they offer no spontaneous help to one's self-centered feelings, one's egoistic longing, but speak rather of the certainty of destiny. The hour of death is never a mistake, but enacted in clear consequence of the person's karma.

Especially where death occurs due to an accident, this reassurance is needed, because the *ifs* and *buts* of the fatal few seconds that bring about a collision on the road are endless, however futile.

I therefore quote from one of the addresses given by Rudolf Steiner in response to this question.

My dear friends, it is infinitely important that we gradually develop in our souls a feeling for the effective wisdom of the world, and that we permeate ourselves fully with this feeling. When this feeling increasingly permeates man, it will lead to an ability to accept destiny and all the blows of destiny, which without this trust would be very hard to bear.

If one is able to observe the spiritual worlds in which the dead dwell, one may very often see that it is easiest for the dead if those whom they have left behind on the earth themselves trust in this wisdom.

Certainly it is understandable that we weep for our dead, but it signifies doubt in this wisdom if we cannot get beyond the weeping—and he who can see into the spiritual worlds knows that the wish that the dead might not have died, might still be here and not in the spiritual world, disconcerts the dead most of all. We can greatly lighten up life after death for the dead if we can accept our destiny and think about the dead in such a way that we know that the wielding wisdom has wanted to take him from us at the right hour, because it needed him in other spheres of existence. So much will depend on this, that in the future man will be able in a greater degree to work into what constitutes human suffering on earth in a helpful way—but that it will also be quite clear that there is the working of karma, and that if death comes to one we love, it was a karmic necessity.

This will hinder no one from doing everything possible for the person while he is still alive, provided it is done with the right attitude. But, as human beings, we may in a way not think beyond what is given to us, and it must be clear that the all-powerful wisdom of the world is after all wiser than we are. What I have said seems almost banal, simplistic, common truth and trivial, but it exists so little in our time. Infinite happiness would come to the dead and to the living if it were more readily known, if it would pervade our souls as an attitude, and if the human souls could think of the dead as being alive, think of them reaching into the physical life on earth; this is so important.[5]

I read and re-read those words over and over again.

As I write this I am aware that the way to find help is very different for different people. Even the four sets of parents involved in the very same accident had to look for individual explanations in order to discern some meaning in what had happened.

My attempt is merely to share—with whoever may need it—my experiences, my sources of support, as in my case very few people had anything to suggest at all. Conventional prayer may help some, if they are still firmly rooted in a strong faith. For others, it will be hard to find any words to utter, not knowing which ones and to whom to direct them. Death as an experience is too uncompromising, too desperate, and too final.

The cry that is known to anyone who has experienced such a loss is, Where are you? How can I reach you? How can I know that I *can* reach you, and that you can reach me? What can I *do* for you?

Someone said to me, "Try to become very calm, very still." It is true, this is essential, otherwise all one experiences is one's own feelings, one's own remorse over shortcomings towards the other, one's own unwillingness to accept or to let go. And that of course leaves little room for the much subtler experiencing of the one who has died. It effectively blocks it out.

However, the pain is justified. We need to feel it. Rudolf Steiner speaks of it as follows:

Now it is not at all the same whether a soul passes through the gate of death in relatively early years or later in life. The death of young children who have loved us is a very different thing from the death of people older than ourselves. Experience of the spiritual world discovers that the secret of communion with children who have died can be expressed by saying that in a spiritual sense we do not lose them, they remain with us. When children die in early life, they continue to be with us— spiritually with us. I should like to give it to you as a theme for meditation, that when little children die they are not lost to us; we do not lose them, they stay with us spiritually. Of older people who die the opposite may be said. Those who are older do not lose us. *We* do not lose children; elderly people do not lose *us*. When elderly people die, they are strongly drawn to the spiritual world, but this also gives them the power so to work into the physical world that it is easier for them to approach us. True, they withdraw much further from the physical world than do children who remain near us, but they are endowed with higher faculties of perception than children who die young. Knowledge of different souls in the spiritual world reveals that those who die in old age are able to enter easily into the souls on earth; they do not lose the souls on earth. And we do not lose little children, for they remain more or less within the sphere of earthly man. The meaning of the difference can also be considered from another aspect.

We do not always have sufficiently deep insight into the experiences of the soul on the physical plane. When friends die, we mourn and feel pain. When good friends pass away, I have often said that it is not the task of anthroposophy to offer people shallow consolation for their pain, or to try to talk them out of their sorrow. One should grow strong enough to bear sorrow; not allow oneself to be talked out of it. But people make no distinction as to whether the sorrow is caused by the death of a child or of one who is elderly. Spiritually perceived, there is a very great difference. When children die, the pain of those who have remained behind is really a kind of compassion—no matter whether those children were their own, or other children whom they loved. Children remain with us and because we have been united with them, they convey their pain to our souls; we feel their pain —that they would fain still be here! Their pain is eased when we bear it with them. The child feels in us, shares his feeling with us, and it is good that it is so; his pain is thereby lessened, relieved a little.

On the other hand, the pain we feel at the death of older people, whether relatives or friends, can be called egoistic pain. An elderly person who has died does not lose us, and the feeling he has is therefore different from the feeling present in a child. We here in life feel that we have lost him—the pain is therefore *ours,* it is egoistic pain. We do not share in his feeling as we do in the case of children; we feel the pain for ourselves.

A clear distinction can therefore be made between

these two forms of pain: egoistic pain in connection with the elderly; pain filled with compassion in connection with children. The child lives on in us and we actually feel what he feels. In reality, our own soul mourns only for those who die in the later years of their life.[6]

This means that the pain we experience upon the death of a child is very different from the sorrow we feel for an older person. The pain we feel for a child is *her* pain, it is *her* anguish of soul, because she would fain be living still! This belief puzzled me a lot. How can a soul-spirit, having been freed from physical-sensory confines, feel pain? Is she not now in the presence of wisdom and love, understanding all things, even the rightness of her own death?

Gradually I grasped that there is indeed a difference between soul and spirit. In how many cases in our lives do we profoundly know that a particular event or incident is right; it had to happen in a particular way no matter how painful. Our spirit knows! However, our soul follows, often reluctantly, and often it suffers a great deal along the way. So it must be then for the soul of a young child who was torn from life. The young child wants to accomplish so many things. She is full of the desire to grow and to experience the fullness of life on earth. To experience its colors, riches, joys, and involvements. Suddenly, the child is bereft of it all!

The soul of a child is close to ours! Her pain is *our* pain, our suffering is *her* suffering! To see this helps to transform our sorrow into active, compassionate love. Once again, especially in the evenings before we go to sleep, we can open our arms, our heart, and embrace our child, comforting her pain. During the day I believe that one can continue to talk quite normally with one's child. We may look for appropriate words, prayers or

13

verses, feeling that our usual words are too simple. We can take her along, saying (perhaps inaudibly), "Come, let us go for a walk," or "See how beautiful the day is today," or even "Dear love, forgive me—I must cry." Allow the soul of the child to live with you, because she will look for closeness to you, her mother, as no one belongs so intimately to her as you do. She is connected to you by bonds of karma and destiny. The suffering you experience is *your mutual* destiny.

There is something one can do. There are the nights.

During the day we, the so-called living, are separated. Our bodies confine us within our sensory experiences. The body is in the way; it blocks out the finer sensations, as the sun blocks out the stars during the day. But during the night we can be sure to be in that spiritual world where our beloved child lives. Especially in the first weeks and months after death, we are sure to meet, to encounter one another, to be together. This may not always be remembered the next day, because our ordinary consciousness and memory are geared only to the experiences in the physical-sensory world, and we must accept this.

When we go to sleep, we are so close! We may fall asleep with the wish, the plea, "Let us be together; let me find you." We may want to take with us gifts, loving gratitude, images of beauty, and arms full of roses in our soul!

Dreams may seem like a reflection of the meeting. Their imagery, once again, is liable to be earthly. They are merely like the garments of a person. The real encounter is even closer.

We may wake up at peace, restored to some extent. Calm. However, every morning we must face the agonizing facts of the earthly separation again!

The nights take on quite a new reality. Previously,

14

they may have been restful, a blank, little thought about part of our life. Now they become a realm with its own reality.

Perhaps we may sense that the impact of taking any pain killer or sleeping pill will cloud the ability to perceive. In my own experience, this was certainly the case. I took a pain killer for a headache just once. I recall clearly that it took several hours until I felt clear again. It was as if a heavy curtain had come down inwardly, blocking off all finer sensation and making my perception immobile and foggy.

One learns to live with one's soul, because with its help one reaches out and seeks to accompany the child who has gone, or, rather, gone ahead.

Each mother will find her own words—words that belong to her special child, maybe the prayer the child used to say. I want to share here some verses and prayers given by Rudolf Steiner to those who asked him for such help. They can be used in this sequence—as the immediacy of the death experience recedes—but really, as the need arises.

> Divine in my Soul, to you I shall give space
> In the conscious part of my being:
> You bind me to everything
> That the power of destiny has brought to me;
> You never sever me from that which you have
>   given me to love:
> Your spirit watches over what is mine, because it
>   is also yours:
> Thus I shall wake with you, through you, in you.
> What you have concluded with what is yours
> I will be strong enough to accept, that it be wisdom.

> God's wisdom doth order the World
> It orders also me; In it I will live.

God's love doth warm the World
It warmeth also me; In it I will breathe.

God's strength doth bear the World
It beareth also me; In it I will think.

One may wish to extend this last prayer-like verse,
which can give so much inner support, and reassures
one of not having fallen from God's hands, that is, from
God's order, love, and strength. One may perhaps extend it to include the beloved other one, and develop it
further:

God's wisdom doth order the World
It orders also me—it orders also you
In it I will live—may you live in God's order.

God's love doth warm the World
It warmeth also me—it warmeth also you
In it I will breathe—may you breathe in God's love.

God's strength doth bear the World
It beareth also me—it beareth also you
In it I will think—
May you, in thinking, perceive the World that is
around you now.

3

Help We Can Give

As a mother you may feel as I did. When Saskia died, I asked, "Who is taking care of you now?" When I confided this to a learned man, he said to me, "This is just foolish."

It took years to grasp that Saskia existed before she came into my care. She had been cared for and guided into her incarnation. Soon I began to realize that we are all cared for, either in this world or in another. If this were not so, we would be incapable of living, or even merely being. Accepting that this is the case, perhaps it is not only our own desire to *do* something, to continue to help and care, but perhaps it is also the very child in our soul who asks for help. What can we do to help?

First, we must not forget the child who has died. Not even try to forget. Not even think about forgetting, even if the circumstances are painful. Who of us would want that to happen to us, even if we were only to go as far away as another country on earth? We continue to exist, and we hope to be remembered.

When the soul enters death, Rudolf Steiner explains, it is not easy for the soul to comprehend the new environment. Especially in a sudden death, without a moment's warning or preparation. It is plummeted into a world that has no physical-sensory reality. Our sense organs, which gave us the experiences of the physical world, have been left behind in the physical body that has been cast off and can no longer be used. All we have now are our memory pictures. They appear to us and help us to be aware of ourselves as a self. However, they are made of a substance that resembles our dream pictures. They are not hard and fast and sure but float into our awareness and disappear again, like disconnected fragments or drifting cloud formations. Here we can help the child's soul. We can try to link these fragments, by carefully *re-membering* what we have experienced together. Steadily, we can retrace our child's life, forming clear images, seeing them and connecting them. We may sit down and write the story of our child's life by chronicling backward as she is now doing. In fact, we may wish to add a thought, a loving message here or there. It may be painful to recall the special incidents of a happy holiday, a quiet evening together, or even moments of impatience. It is important to weave the incidents together, bit by bit, and to connect individual events with a thread of love and gratitude. Love and gratitude must be communicated throughout. This will help to create the sheaths for the child's soul in the soul-world. The child may read together with us, read and remember by the reflections and the images in our soul. So much has remained unsaid; so much has remained undone!

Thus to remember can be of real help to the soul of the child who needs to find a new orientation. And it can be of great comfort for us to be able to do something for her and with her.

Sometimes doubt may arise. Am I not deceiving myself? How can I know that he or she is really being reached? A passage like the following, sent to me by a dear and knowing friend, often helped me.

> . . . And it is truly so that all that has been woven between souls who met in their physical existence here

on earth is laid down. What we experienced as loving relationships, what we encountered in friendships or as otherwise related people, what we experienced through physical impressions in a physical body, we lay down, give up, as we lay down the physical body itself. But through the fact that we have developed relationships with family, through friendships or love, something is transplanted into what builds up a future life beyond the portal of death in the spiritual world.

We do not only labor by ourselves, but already in the time during which we undergo the moral evaluation of our past life we work together with those human souls whom we loved and valued in this world.

All this becomes real knowledge through exact clairvoyance and does not remain subject to faith alone. It enters the immediate vision (*Anschauung*) of man.

Yes, we may even say that here in the physical world there is an abyss between souls, however much they may love each other, because they meet within the limits of their bodily existences, and these can enter only into such interrelationships as are possible through bodily encounters. But when the human being is in the spiritual world, then it is not so that the body of a person he loved is an obstacle to living closely with the other person's soul.

As one can acquire the ability to look through physical objects into the spiritual realm, in like manner the one who has gone through the portal of death has the ability to perceive and communicate with the souls he has left behind, overcoming the barriers of the physical body. He experiences them still as souls, as long as they are on earth, up until their own death.[1]

During the first weeks and months, when suddenly great emptiness and silence irrevocably surrounded me, it was good to find a certain life rhythm in which to turn to my beloved lost companion. In the mornings, when

I had returned from sleep—when as yet no other strong impressions had cluttered up my mind, I consciously took Saskia into my day. I repeated to her our new relationship and my deep sorrow. It is so important to regain this peace of mind, to overcome the desperate abyss, because what we experience and what we feel is directly felt and perceived by the other soul.

She can no longer see our outer physical appearance, but she can perceive whether our soul is darkened by doubt and fear, whether it is in great turmoil or firm and clear and to some extent light. We pay little attention to these states of soul, for sensory appearance is so predominant. But when appearance has fallen away, we have to (by elimination) become sensitive to the coloring and movements of the soul. In his book, *Theosophy*, Rudolf Steiner speaks of "the longing of a human soul appearing here like a gentle sigh; and outbreak of passion is like a stormy blast in the spirit land."[2]

If we have the wish to communicate some special gifts, we must try to create pictures in our own soul. We may want to tell her of something beautiful we have seen, or we may realize that she needs to understand much more about the meaning of Christianity, seeing she left so young—too early to have learned it in life on earth. It is no good just to tell her something, or to read to her. What we want to share must be brought into living images. In our mind we must try to picture to ourselves, for example, the scene of the Sermon on the Mount, the parable of the five barley loaves and two fishes, or the Transfiguration.[3] This takes a real effort, for we are not used to doing this. Our usual understanding is all too intellectual! It is often abstract, formless, and colorless.

If we attempt to do this, we will enter into a new

relationship with our own soul and gradually begin to feel how similarly immaterial the soul is to the existence of our child now.

There is so much she still wanted to experience, to learn and to do! This beautiful verse by Maria Reimann can indicate how we can try to allow the soul to continue to experience through us—at least for a while longer. It can guide us to seek certain experiences, and also to avoid others.[4]

My eyes be unto you, beloved soul, as windows,
That through them you may see the earthly beauty.
My ears be unto you, beloved soul, as doorways, that
Through them in hearing you may enter the ether's weaving realm.

When you behold through my eyes the earthly beings,
Through you I listen upward to the starry courses.
When you, through my listening,
Enter into the weaving-ether-light
Then I behold, through the mirror of your soul,
With mine inner eye the realm of angels.
And the here and the yonder
Find themselves in loving harmony
When the sun is in the center—
When the flame of love glows with sacrifice.

Indeed, a very fine weaving can come about in this way. The child is still so close to us, he or she can perceive through our soul and through our eyes and ears. This was my experience, and I consciously sought out occasions of visual or auditory beauty, a concert or a beautiful flower that would light up my soul, in order to offer it to Saskia. Later I read in Rudolf Steiner that when we send our thoughts and experiences upwards,

21

it is like experiencing the gift of music or of art for the soul that has left her body. It enriches the life of the loved one, just as art and colors enrich our lives.

But we must know of this possibility, and know that it matters; most of us may not know of it, and then cannot try to make this kind of offering.

And *we* can do it. We who are so close with the child as parents or friends. Only we alone to start with, however. Other people are less perceptible to the soul when they are perceived from the other side of reality. A great task is therefore placed upon us, a need only we can fulfill for our child, a task we so gladly accept.

Together with our child, we must slowly transform the despair, the hurt, and the utter loss. Together, we must come to terms with what has happened. If we try, we can be of immense help to our child. We need to mourn, to give time and life to it, and we must suffer, because, as I said before, we experience *her* pain. We need to help her even now, and not burden her by our despair, by *our* bereft feelings, and by our inner resentment of her fate. There is only one thing that will bridge the abyss, will continue in the face of deepest despair, will endure no matter the doubt, anger and loss of reality: love. No thought, no theory, no belief or explanation—only love. Love will slowly pave the way for the rest to follow: the thoughts, beliefs, understandings and, finally, acceptance.

Imbue with your love a verse or a prayer your child may have known well, or think vividly of a situation you have experienced together, for example, a game, a conversation, a precious moment during a holiday, or something you really wanted to do together. Live intensely within that moment. Then you can hope to meet!

What you do during the day, perhaps at regular times, will be carried over into the body-free encounter in the night and will be a gift, a joy, and a support on the way. Take a bowl of roses across each night to your beloved one. But take care to take with you only those things that she can understand now—only those thoughts and feelings imbued with selflessness, above all those that are related to Christ.

4

Reaching Out

It confused me to start with, yes, even annoyed me to some extent, that the verses given by Rudolf Steiner often do not use the direct "I" and "you" form, but rather "we" and "you" in the plural form. The relationship with my child was strictly between her and me. Others—on this or that side—were not a part of that relationship. The memory of that relationship was all there was left to me. This is shown clearly in the following verse by Rudolf Steiner:

> Our love may follow you,
> Soul, that lives in the Spirit
> That beholds your earthly life
> And, thus gazing, knows itself as spirit,
> And what appears to you through thinking
> As your Self in the land of souls,
> May accept our love,
> So that we may feel ourselves in you,
> So that you may find in our souls
> That which lives with you in faithfulness.

I gradually learned and slowly accepted the lesson contained in these very words.

Separateness is real only for the physical, material world. Only for this world is it correct to say that where there is one object, there can be no other. In the soul world, there is no such separation, for thoughts and feelings rise up from seemingly nowhere. Like wafting, or fleeting cloud patches, or streams of warmth or wind, they intermingle. The other soul does not belong to us, as a possession. We can try to look for it, seek it, hope to reach it, but we can never grasp it, hold it, or force it to stay with us exclusively.

I experienced this as a slow and at times painful lesson. Finally, I surrendered, and later on opened my soul positively. It occurred to me that in ordinary life too, love between people can be very selfish and possessive. This kind of love forces the physical presence of the other person in the belief that by doing so we can keep a hold on the other's love; this is, of course, unreal. Love is always a gift. Slowly, the desperate attempt to hang on, to assure oneself of the existence of the other in the realm of supersensible reality, grows into an offering gesture; the hands open up, rather than grasp.

Gradually one accepts and knows in a deeper way that *all* love, not only one's own but that sent by anybody at all, can and will be of help and support. Love can bring light and enrichment to the beloved person. One joins one's own love to the stream of *our* love. When we overcome our selfish hold, what is spoken of in the prayer presented earlier becomes an experience. The soul of the one who has gone from the physical world can be perceived as a sphere around us. As we become aware of this, we realize how careful we must be with our thoughts and feelings, because these soul-forces are effective in this sphere.

An image may rise from the above prayer: the image of an expanded sphere around us that is not, however, spatial, but inward, as a chalice might be. We hope that she can find us like this: that our thoughts may be sustenance to her searching soul. May there be light in our souls, generated by prayer, so that her angel may lead her on and light her way, to where we cannot yet follow. One day we shall.

An old Gaelic prayer, which Saskia often used, speaks of this.

Thou Angel of God, who has charge of me
From the dear Father of mercifulness,
The shepherding King of the fold of the saints,
To make round about me this night;
Surround me on the sea of unrighteousness
And in the narrows, crooks and straights;
Keep thou my coracle, keep it always.

Be thou a bright flame before me—
Be thou a guiding star above me;
Be thou a smooth path below me,
And be a kindly shepherd behind me—
Today, tonight, and forever.

I am tired and I am a stranger
Lead thou me to the land of the angels
For me it is time to go home
To the Court of Christ,
To the peace of heaven.

(collected by Alexander Carmichael in *The Sundancers*)

Perhaps the togetherness of our souls and spirits beyond death is most beautifully described by William Penn:

They that love beyond the world
Cannot be separated by it;
Death cannot kill what never dies,
Nor can spirits ever be divided
That love and live in the same divine principle.

Death is but crossing the world,
As friends do the seas;
They live in one another still—
They live in one another still . . .

The words of the Gospel of John, or other spiritual
writings, if allowed to live in our soul, can be food for
one who wanders in the land of truth, and in the land-
scapes of the spirit.

I took Saskia strongly into my mind, into my heart-
warmed thoughts, and bid her be beside me as I read
to her in my thoughts. It needed much concentration
to do this, as the ability to hold fast to such a situation
was, to start with, very limited.

The will is not accustomed to travel inward; it is too
weak to sustain good intentions for long. We slacken,
we doubt, we give up. But we should never cease to
do this deed of love and faithfulness. Rudolf Steiner
said that he had never come across a situation between
souls related in both worlds, where such help was no
longer necessary. But sadly, so he said, people gradually forget. Even for very wise, spiritually advanced,
and learned persons, perhaps much more advanced
than ourselves, this help is still needed.

A friend once told me how her father, a spiritually
advanced, leading personality, had come into her
dreams several years after his death. He asked her why
she had not done anything for him. She had thought
that he would not require such modest assistance as she
felt she could offer. She believed that he would advance
knowingly and easily in the other worlds, which he had
studied and related to so well while living on earth.

The so-called dead need us, and we need them. We
need their guidance, because their vision is so much
freer, and so much more circumspect. And as we our-

selves grow older, the other shore becomes more and more crowded with friends who have gone ahead!

Another aspect to which Rudolf Steiner draws our awareness is that although it is of vital importance whether someone dies young or at an older age (more reference to this in a later chapter), after an initial time we must not apply the terms child or adult any longer. A child was a child to us when on the earth for a short period of time. This definition made him or her a child. He or she was still in a particular stage of incarnation into his or her body and the world, but since this particular bond is dissolved, the being is no longer a child in the soul and spirit world. He or she is a being in his or her own right, on his or her own path of development, through repeated incarnations. This being now sees so much more clearly what is essential for the advance of mankind and for the good of the world. These beings can send us strength. A verse by Rudolf Steiner expresses this:

> Feel how full of love we look towards the heights,
> Which called you forth to other spheres of work.
> Reach out your strength from realms of Spirit
> To your friends who are bereaved;
> Hear the pleading of our souls,
> Sent to follow you in trust.
> We need here, in our work on earth,
> Strong forces from the spirit land,
> Which we owe in thanks to our dead friends.

We can learn to turn to these beings for guidance and help. Open our souls to their ideas and motivations, and to their intentions.

5

What To Do About Belongings Left Behind?

Clothes and toys will not be needed any more by Saskia.

I believe there is a real difference between a child or person who dies gradually, perhaps due to a long illness, and a soul who is torn out of life unprepared, unexpectedly, mercilessly and abruptly. It is for the latter that I make the following suggestions.

We do not only live in our bodies; our belongings and home environment are part of our earthly sheaths, which are not only interwoven with us, but also created and assembled by each person in a unique way. The number of possessions is inconsequential.

We can experience this clearly when coming into someone's room while the owner is not there. The atmosphere belongs to the owner. This is also pertinent when we treasure a gift especially because it has belonged to someone we love or revere.

I feel one should only gradually disperse and remove earthly sheaths. Not for the sake of hanging on to outer things, but because it took some time to assemble them. Each item has a meaning in the loved one's life. One may cherish each for a while, perhaps even in the same place, for as one sees these items, and turns to them gently, they may even tell one a little more about the departed. For example, what her particular concerns, inclinations, hobbies, or pastime joys were. These treasures lie ownerless now, unneeded, and unwanted. Perhaps one feels an inner strain of pain and remorse because one took too little time and interest in the general bustle of life to really care for what mattered to the one who is gone.

I believe it is important to allow a little time. How long may be very individual, and will depend on the circumstances as well as on the relationship between the individuals involved.

I think that the hasty dispersal, the sharing and passing on to others, the tidying up, and perhaps throwing away can wait a little, perhaps several weeks. It is not helpful to the departed if it is all dispersed too quickly, just as little as it is good to leave it all untouched for years, making a monument of what was once a living environment, a colorful and changeable sheath.

It will surely mean a great deal to the departed soul if we lovingly look back with her to her treasured belongings: maybe a special toy animal, a tennis racquet, some shells gathered for their beauty during a holiday and witness to a happy stroll along a beach. As we see and touch them, they become milestones along the journey she is now travelling back to the beginning. Her schoolbooks deserve loving care also. How much toil and effort, probably at times anguish, but also joyful pride, went into them. Little else received such constant, lasting attention. The books create an image of her writing. We can sense when she was feeling happy and well, when she was tired, or when she was in a hurry to finish, in order to go our and play. She speaks to us through these images. Perhaps it pains us to think that we didn't help her more, or that we gave her too little encouragement. It burns in our soul, and we may whisper: *Please, love, forgive me.*

It is in a mood of caring that I feel it is right not to disregard these little belongings. For example, some special clothes she considered her favorites. She wore them until they became too small and discolored from wear, but she loved them. Perhaps the occasion will arise when we may pass some of them on to a friend, someone who may either really need them, or to whom they may give joy because she or he knew the child and some of her things can now live on.

Often we may find that there is no one who wants these possessions. Then, after a time (we will somehow feel when), we may decide to burn some of the belongings, not in a mood of desperate realism, thinking that they are useless, but rather accepting that our beloved child has other cares and joys now. We merely help her to tidy up what she had no time to do herself.

Although it is a very different thing, I want to add the consideration of the graveside. It is true that we cannot look for the living friend in the other world of existence at the graveside. But a grave is a help in many ways. One can go there. One can *do* something, such as planting flowers and bushes, tending them, watering them, seeing them grow, and even, if you like, showing them to the child: *See how beautifully they bloom for you.*

Although it is painful, to stand at the graveside is needed, because what we face goes totally beyond our understanding, our possibility to follow, and our ability to think. It is fathomless. But we may try again and again to tell ourselves in a prayer-like way that what lies buried is only the physical sheath, which has been laid aside, hurt, destroyed and no longer usable.

Even the anger we may feel, the well-nigh hatred that may rise up at whoever caused this accident to happen, this anger or hatred needs to be transformed, overcome, lifted up, offered up, and forgiven. Together we may be able to do this. It may take months and years, but on it depends much for the living, light-filled freedom of our dearest child. On it depends whether our soul will become stony, hard and bitter, whether it will form a rigid scar over the terrible wound that we share, or whether it will heal.

All too many people dare not, cannot go through this process, either because the pressures of daily life over-burden them all too soon, or because there is no one to help them to know how to think, and how to bridge the deep abyss between a happy life together and this earthbound silence.

Trying to forget is no answer. We cannot forget. We may suppress, push it aside out of the mind, but this can only lead to uncertainty in our relationship to a spiritual existence and guidance. We all must accept the irreversible might of God's will. How we do it, how-ever, is an individual matter.

God has given to us before he took away. The pervad-ing feeling in our soul must gradually become *gratitude* for what was once ours to love and care for.

Love and gratitude, these will in time overcome and transform remorse and loss. Considerations like these may be thought and experienced time and again at the graveside. These words were formulated by myself, but they express the way through the kingdoms of Nature and Man—up to the soul and spirit world. A kind of inner ladder I speak of later.

> We may try to think
> How the physical body has returned to the earth—
> How the warm life, once quickening that body,
> can be seen as the living breath in all plants around
>   us,
> in all that is alive around us—

How a living soul filled the body with joy and pain,
and gave form to it.
All these were permeated by God's universal spirit.
How man is called to lift himself up
and re-unite with the divine.

We may then, having lovingly gone through these
thoughts step by step, raise our head and lift up our
gaze to the open sky above us.

How the soul guides her flight into the heights
and experiences deep devoutness now;
How the eternal I in each man unites again
with the eternal well-spring of God's Word,
and how, freed from all bondage,
the spirit streams in the light around the earth,
Christ's light.

The abyss between the earth's existence and the
realm of God is too far apart; the gap is too wide. Our
soul is too sad and too heavy to cross it in one leap. To
go step by step as on an inner ladder is a help. It may
take time, and our feelings may wish to ever again wash
over such a path, but if we attempt to understand bit
by bit then the gap will be transformed and we will feel
lighter and freer each time we try.

In old paintings, especially by Fra Angelico and others, this image is presented. The women stand at the
empty grave; they are looking downward into the
grave. They are sorrowful. Above them, right over the
grave in subtle dimensions of light, cloud and color,
appears the Risen Christ. But they, like we, are captives
of their downward glance.

Together, we go the way, we try to accept, try to
accompany, and try to follow.

6

Did You Experience Her?

"Did you experience her?" people have often asked me when they wanted to express more than mere sympathy. "Did you feel her? Could you sense her being near you?" they have questioned further.

These questions presuppose the acceptance that in fact Saskia continued to exist—despite her absence from visibility. They were always difficult to answer. I wanted to say, "Yes" and describe for them my sense of Saskia. Was this not precisely what I longed for, pleaded for and waited for?

I received the most beautiful letters from a few friends, who wrote that they had seen her in certain situations, together with someone else who had also died. They were now walking together. "He had taken her by the hand," they explained, and she was learning new things. Someone else saw her go forward courageously and joyfully.

I raised the question, Did they really see her? Had this friend a capacity to see what was seemingly closed to me? Or was it my friend's vivid imagination that saw Saskia in secure, positive company? Perhaps these possibilities were in reality much closer than one normally would consider. Where did reality begin and end?

One of the other parents who had lost a child in the same accident knew a woman who had second sight. This lady had seen our children. She described them fairly accurately; she had not known them when they were alive. It was a straw to cling to—maybe materialistic—a definite proof that one's belief in spirituality was as yet too weak. Although I had no intention to involve my dear child in any forceful interference from this side, as it were to call her back to visibility, I could not resist the temptation to go to this lady, who had, as I said, the ability to see the unseen, and to predict a bit of the future. I felt like Thomas, the Doubter, who had to see in order to believe, but my own reality had been thoroughly shattered. Any kind of certainty would be of assistance.

I tried to be calm and open. The woman, after a while, said, "Yes, I can see her. She is standing right next to you. She is looking at you. You must not weep and grieve too much. It makes her sad, and weighs her down. It slows her down in making her way upwards into the higher spheres."

It all made sense. Then, when the woman began to talk about my father and mother, the information was confused and incorrect. We ended the session by agreeing that the people who had died were alive in another world. I left her; I did not ask the questions I had so desperately wanted to ask. During the entire time, I was aware that I was a pupil of Rudolf Steiner. I knew the answers. It was really not for me to seek this kind of reassurance. What I did not know, I had to work out inwardly by myself.

I mention this visit, because the attempt to seek confirmation in a more tangible form is all too human and understandable. It did no harm, but merely left me to proceed by myself.

Several friends, who were living in Germany, in England, and in South Africa, wrote that they had experienced Saskia in their dreams. I want to share part of a very special letter that gave me great comfort. It was written by someone who had never written a letter like this before and has not since. Her other letters had, at all times, dealt only with the practical, social aspects of life.

I have seen Saskia on a beach, free as the wind and reveling in being no longer "of the earth." She was so happy and gay.... Some friends, who have also known your Saskia, have told me or written that they too had some kind of experience of her, and they live all over the world now. But each independent person's story had the same quality: that Saskia is happy and unafraid ... but I think that God had called Saskia earlier, because He needed her to help Him. She has touched so many people by her death in a pure and beautiful way.... She has not gone very far. She is in your heart and in the hearts of everyone who knew and loved her and liked her. She lives in spirit, free as the wind, and God will bless her.

As the letter came on Christmas day—it was my first one alone—it was like a message from Saskia.

In order to tell the whole story—so that it can possibly be of help to others—I must write that I was given the most wonderful help by many, many dreams. I never dreamed of her while she was alive. I seldom dream of people or circumstances connected with my immediate daily life or environment.

I mentioned earlier how the nights were the times when I felt I could link up with her most easily—most likely. I spoke about my dreams to no one, lest by talking about them I might harden the experiences, and also dispel them.

Saskia and I lived together in these dreams. It would be too personal to relate the dreams in any detail. Of general interest perhaps is that our contact was very, very close, much closer in fact than it had been during her earthly life. In the sequence of these dreams, which lasted for about ten months after her death, she changed from the actual age and size she had been at the time of her departing, thirteen, to becoming younger—only a babe in my arms. In the last dreams, however, she was older again. She seemed older and wiser than she had been in life. The dreams contained aspects of Saskia's life—what she had liked and enjoyed doing, especially horseback riding. The dreams were always in unfamiliar surroundings; they were in no way a part of my own recollections.

It is with hesitation that I offer some of my dream experiences. If I do it, it is because I remember my own anguish, my desperate search for anything that could give me reassurance, tangibly, of the continued existence of my child.

This, I know, is what every parent feels, and yet it is mostly referred to in only very vague terms, such as: "She has gone to heaven. One day you will meet her there."

Where, then, is that heaven?

Did my dreams perhaps reach into a spiritual sphere, where the souls of the so-called dead are? Is there a reality in the words, "Death is a long sleep; sleep is a shorter death," or "Sleep is a brother to death?" Did people in earlier times perhaps know more of such things? Have we lost such deeper knowledge?

At a very early stage, I had a dream of which I will only tell the significant parts. We were together in a town, and we were on our way home. I seemed to be in a hurry, as, alas, I was so often. There were many people. Saskia said, "Wait for me, wait. You are moving too fast." I walked on, trying to go into the light on the other side of the road between trees, so that she could see me better and follow; then I awoke, and she had stayed behind. I was filled with the experience of having been with her; I had gone on, and woken up in the sunlit, sensory world into which she could no longer follow.

Do we know where our soul is when we sleep? Into what spheres it enters?

Another time, we were together in a mountainous landscape. Saskia moved so lightly, up and up, jumping fearlessly over crevices. I, on the other hand, climbed with much effort, full of anxiety over slipping and falling. Saskia moved ahead. She seemed to move weightlessly, to and fro on pathways of rays of light, and she was so joyful. I awoke deeply comforted, filled with joy and peace and gratitude that she had been so happy. It was also shown to me that I had to use quite different perspectives in order to comprehend the new dimensions in which she was now. It was often difficult to translate what was conveyed into my ordinary earthly thinking.

I hasten to say that I have no psychic tendencies whatsoever in everyday life, but clearly the intense pain had opened up my soul for a short span of time. It was through this that I was able to recall the images and words clearly, although there were also areas that I could not recall on waking up. On reading this, some mothers may think, "I did not dream in such a way. Why was I unable to meet?" I would like to suggest that we all can meet, we all *do* meet, but we cannot always remember it. It may be that we need to go to sleep with an open mind. It was also a definite experience for me, time and again, that it was in fact *my* darkness, *my* despair, *my* anger and sorrow, that weighed me down and closed me off.

Similar to the way in which I had experienced a counterimpact on my consciousness when taking painkillers,

41

as described earlier, I now avoided all film shows and television. These have a strong cluttering effect on one's soul-mirror, if I may call it that. And if the much subtler imagery of dreams was to appear, I had to keep this inner "screen" clear and clean. It goes without saying that alcohol has a similar effect on blurring the clarity of the soul's perceptiveness.

Ultimately, though, I believe that dreams that give comfort and evidence are a gift. One cannot force them to be given; one can only be grateful.

Between our together-dreams, I had dreams of a more general, spiritual nature, certain brief "teachings" one might say. In these my child had no part. They were images or events in other circumstances. At first they were purely visual, mostly in color; later they included audible sentences. The intensity of these dreams was such that I had no difficulty in remembering, re-seeing them in my mind, and I could write them down.

It is not the purpose of this book to relate the content of these more objective spiritual experiences. I mention only one which remained a challenging thought long after the dreams had ceased to come. It said that "we must learn that between the living-visible and the working reality of the creative force there is no clear, definite borderline."

Could this mean that we must learn to seek the spiritual *in* the world around us, not "behind the clouds," and that the souls of the so-called dead are around us, in our souls, and not far away? I write this not because I want to lay any stress at all on the content or message of dream experiences, but merely to point to the fact that they prove that we live and experience differently in different states of consciousness.

We all know that we are pretty helpless in making up our own dreams. We may ardently wish to dream about a certain thing, or perhaps avoid it; however, it is not in our conscious power to create our dreams.

Although in looking back, I can say that I was helped existentially by these dreams, they did not take away the horrific pain. At the same time, my physical and my soul's pain—of great intensity—lasted for two to three years. Regular bouts of despair entered my life. Only tears helped these.

I would like to mention something else that was a very special sphere of experience for me during the first months and years. It was the sphere of church services. Maybe it is equally obscure and understandable that I found myself helplessly overcome by tears each time I went to a church service. To start with, I could not manage to listen beyond the Gospel reading without weeping, no matter how hard I tried. Much later, when I had virtually overcome this, the church services continued to be a time during which strong feelings concerning Saskia welled up in my soul. Was this because a kind of threshold situation regarding the spiritual is an intrinsic part of each church service? Was it because in the Christian Community service, in the Act of Consecration of Man, the souls of the dead are consciously included as if they were present and were partaking in the offering?

At one time an older friend who through her spiritual steadfastness had been a great support to me—she was ever ready to change my doubt into trusting hope—said to me, "Why are you weeping? Saskia is sitting at your side spiritually." This was by no means meant as a spiritist vision. It was intended to be spiritually real and true at the occasion of the service.

Perhaps I had to cry in that situation so much and for so long because Saskia was indeed particularly close to me then. Today I am sure that this was so. It was as if my soul resembled a hard stone that could only be worn down by tears. I knew it quite well and said it to myself: "As long as you still need to cry, you have not achieved the necessary real love in order to let Saskia be free. Let go of the strong, inner clinging to her. Allow her to go her way, to follow her path of destiny that might reach far beyond your life span."

And still, many years later, my tears rise inwardly at the occasion of special services. I sometimes consider that this happens when Saskia's soul comes close to my soul; gently it approaches, helps, redeems, and asks, "Has your soul now become wide enough? Have you true love?" The tears last so long till the soul—or is it the heart?—becomes transparent and clean. This clarity creates a still and peaceful surface on which the loved soul of our child can appear, like the image of a golden evening sun in the mirror of a still lake.

I must make it clear that Saskia, my only child, had been a strong, healthy, positive, and cheerful child. She was very normal; she had no tendencies towards being hypersensitive or a little unearthly. She loved her life, enjoyed all she did, was positive and tolerant towards all people and events. Indeed, these particular attributes were needed in her life; as the daughter of a mother who pioneered the development of a Camphill Therapeutic Community for mentally handicapped children in South Africa, life was often very demanding and difficult for Saskia.

One quality she had above all, I think, was her fairness to others. She would pursue an issue of right or wrong with ardent persistence. She was modest in her personal wishes and needs, and outgoing to all people and animals.

I remember Saskia, who cried very rarely, twice crying bitterly over seemingly small incidents, but which were so important to her warm heart. Once was when I collected her from an agreed meeting point in town, after she had spent the night with a friend. I found her in front of a shop, dissolved in desperate tears. Only gradually did she calm down sufficiently to be able to speak. In front of the shop, a blind man had been sitting on the pavement, begging. The people had all passed by, nobody had given him anything. Please, could we go back and give him whatever we had? After that, we never passed by a blind beggar again.

There was another incident. One evening we had one of our rare suppers alone together. Saskia was crying. I could think of a good many reasons, such as too little attention, but slowly and reluctantly she told me what was causing her such grief. A duck was sitting in the stables with a broken wing. She would have to suffer all night! Who would notice it and help her now?

Apart from her classmates, Saskia had a special friend. She used to take her pony, Tanglefoot, several kilometers up into the open fields behind Cresset in order to visit this friend. He was an old African, who had his kraal up there. There was a wonderful friendship between this old man and the young girl. Saskia never failed to bring back a present for him from her holidays, such as a pocket knife or some chocolate. Unfortunately he was ill at the time of her accident and could not come to her funeral. He died some months later.

Working in a charitable organization, we never had much money. Saskia wanted to ride in a *gymkhana*. It was to take place at a fair distance away. No problem. Saskia got up at four in the morning, got her horse ready and rode the fifteen kilometers to the meet. All other participants had brought their horses in horseboxes. Of course, her horse was tired, and the only prize she won was for the willingness of her mount on the obstacle course. At the end of the day, she had to ride home again, this time through soaking rain. There was not a word of complaint, just happiness at having been a part of it all.

Saskia was never bored. The days were never long enough for all she wanted to do!

7

Can You Feel Her?

Some people have described that a peculiar sensation of warmth may arise after one has turned to a soul. This usually happens when one has sent a prayer-like offering.

One needs to become more sensitive to a soul in a *real* way, not in obscure psychic sentimental ways. We must be sensitive to the very soul that lives in ourselves. We take so many things for granted without considering how they play into our inner experience. Surely we realize the loved one can no longer appear to us in hard and defined contours. But she may dwell momentarily in a shaft of light falling through our window, in the song of a bird that reaches our ear, or in a gentle wind that touches us as it whispers through the branches of a tree. God's messengers have long been described as having their abode in light and air, and in the quickly changing and dissolving forms that are created in the fine spray of a waterfall, or mist over the sea. Why should this be so mysterious? If we are perceptive, every sensory perception can lead to an experience in our soul. We know this well from music. The vibrations of strings playing together give us the joy of listening to a symphony by Beethoven, or a string quartet by Schubert. These touch our soul, play upon it, lighten it, or make it sad and melancholy. This kind of communion between the sensory world and the soul goes on unnoticed all the time. It is taken for granted, and no one considers it mystical. It simply illustrates the way we are integrated, finely interwoven, and incarnated into this sensory world.

I believe that the soul of the other one, the beloved friend, no longer has the possibility to hear music as we hear it. Her sensory organs are no longer available to her; therefore, we can say, "May my ears be portals to thee." What can be perceived is not the usual music, but the movement this music gently creates in the soul, its shades of light and darkness, its colorful play, and its reflection on the surface of our soul.

But to make it available to the beloved friend, to take her along gently, always in a gesture of offering—if you like, come with me—requires a new kind of hearing, and a different kind of seeing.

To practice some painting, or, however simple, some music—even a melody on a recorder played with ensouled breath—can help one to begin to experience what is perceived.

A gentle interweaving can be experienced. This may help us to begin to appreciate what Rudolf Steiner means when he suggests that it may be of true inner service to the departed to read to him or her. Reading, not as an intellectual activity, but as one in which the word has been raised to an artistic experience, one that is strongly felt and imbued with understanding.

It is not reciting that is meant here, although the reading may be gently audible. One should create an image of what one reads, and choose texts that allow for this—perhaps the Gospels, or descriptions of the departed soul's path into the spiritual world, such as those in Rudolf Steiner's works. One should imagine oneself reading to a specific friend, and continue only for as long as one is capable of truly being aware of the departed person. This, borne by love, can be perceived by the soul of our friend.

Again and again we must make it clear to ourselves that separation is only material—only a physical reality. Every piece of music shows us how a wonderful interweaving of tones and rhythms create the wholeness we then experience. The colors in a picture, or the lines and contours of a piece of sculpture—together, they are creation! And in its highest form it is a multitude of different qualities working together in a human body: we are, each one of us, God's creation.

Rudolf Steiner advises that it does not matter at which hour of the day we do our reading or praying. In the very moment we fall asleep it will be taken with us through the portal into the soul-spirit world that we enter at that point. And we should bring our gift on the wings of love and gratitude.

We must thank our departed loved one for the special moments and events we experienced together, the joys of being together, and the deeds or words of kindness. We must accept that he or she has now died, and that the guiding angel of life and destiny has led him or her to further tasks in the fulfillment of his or her destiny. We must accept the integrity of the "otherness" that may at times seem millions of miles and years away. Slowly our acceptance will transform this otherness into a new togetherness that can embrace all distance, a togetherness that will be beyond separation in space and time. Love alone can expand our soul to the width of the spirit.

Consciously we learn to enter into the landscape of the earthly day and into the sphere of souls' existence of the night. We can take gentle questions with us into sleep, and we *may* receive answers that will seem to be clothed in our own words. Seemingly our own ideas, they can light up within us, helping us to solve a particular problem, or developing a new social form.

Rudolf Steiner describes it so beautifully: "We must learn to hear the other one's words in our own questions."

Let us consider that someone loses a precious relative. The relative, say, dies fairly early, so that the one who is left behind has to complete a long life without him. We see that in considering such a thought something comes before our eyes that is certain to be a question of destiny for many people. What matters now is that spiritual science really can throw light on such questions of destiny. Certainly each case is very different. But just in considering specific situations one receives a certain insight into the mysterious course of human life. For instance, one can have the following experience:

A human being has died fairly early. He has thus been torn away from his family. Through the fact that certain relationships had come about while being together in the physical bodies, connections developed that extended far beyond what could be realized while in the physical world. While living together for ten, twenty, thirty, or forty years a much wider sphere of community between two people is created than can be fully realized in these years. Looking at this from a spiritual-scientific point of view, one can see that the necessary continuation is apparent out of its inner nature, for both the one who stayed behind as well as for the one who has passed through the portal of death into the spiritual. The one who remained has to suffer the loss—he has, so to speak, lost a precious human being out of his field of vision, at a point in time when he did not expect it. Hopes for a further life together in the physical world have been shattered; certain conditions for life have been severed. All this belongs to the life experiences, they all belong closely together with the experiences one has had together while being together in the physical body.

That sorrow and pain when added to these experiences has a changing effect on those connections that began in the physical is clear, because just as everything we experience with each other in daily life on earth works into the stream of evolution, there is added everything that is now being lived through under the impact of the loss. Every sensation, every feeling that is experienced, is added to that which we have lived through together in physical life on earth. This is seen from the point of view of the one who has remained in the physical world.

The point of view of the one who has gone into the spiritual world is very different. He is by no means less together with the one he has left behind. Yes, the one who can investigate such situations with spiritual sight sees clearly that for the one who has gone the conscious togetherness with the souls of those left behind is actually much more intense, much more inwardly close than was ever possible here in the physical body. However, one very often notices that this closer relationship belongs to the completion of the inner relationship that had begun in the physical world.

With the help of positive investigation one can make the following discovery. One can see that people have found each other here in the physical life, and that through this a certain area of mutual interest was formed below the threshold of consciousness. If these people had been together for a longer time in the physical world, the connection that came about on the basis of karma from a former life would not have been able to reach the necessary intensity and depth.

The one who has gone through the portal of death is able during the time in which he is in unison with the souls of those left behind, penetrating and flowing through their thoughts, to bring about the necessary deepening of karma, which he would not have been able to do in life.

Thus, it often belongs to the completion of karma,

that on the one hand pain is suffered, while on the other hand the intensified togetherness with the thoughts of the one left behind can come about.[1]

To end this chapter, it may be right to add yet another perspective to our considerations. Rudolf Steiner says that our ability to change anything in our karma is immobilized once we pass through the gate of death. Everything we have done, said, or left undone, remains, as it were, fixed in that position like an unfinished painting, the brush now having been taken away.

For mutual relationships between people once they are both in the soul-spirit world, this is the same: they cannot change anything then—however much they may wish to—out of their new and more enlightened insight. It requires a new incarnation to undo, to transform, and to change.

But for souls closely related to each other in one life, in the context of whose relationship the one has been called away earlier, it is different. The one who is still on the earth can change, can resolve and work further into a relationship. This throws vital new light on the interdependence between the living and the so-called dead.

. . . And yet another aspect appears if one observes the relationship of the one who follows, as it were, the one who passes later through the portal of death than the one who died earlier. Here one observes that much is ordered differently, depending on the time difference between the two deaths. It is not insignificant when we enter into the spiritual world whether we find a human being there who has died at the same time, or someone who has died perhaps some fifteen years beforehand. By having already spent some time in the spiritual world, that soul has lived through experiences that he now has within him when we finally meet. These work on us and influence us, and thereby the karmic bond is tightened, and that would not have been possible in this way without this time lapse.

We must learn to see everything we thus experience with those that are close to us as grounded in karmic relationships. And even if this cannot relieve us of grief and pain—as I have often said—we can know how everything that happens belongs together. It must nevertheless be said that seen from a certain vantage point life only thus receives its true meaning.

Because it matters that in one human life we live through between death and birth all circumstances and relationships unfold in a way that not merely the parts that belong to this life achieve reality, but also the contributions that this life makes to the following lives on earth to come.

What begins with the painful loss of a relative, or a friend, or someone else close to us, will show its continuation in a next life on earth. And in a certain way all these consequences are already contained in the causes. No loss enters a human life that does not place us rightly into the sequences of earthly lives.

In a specific case this may not engender help in our grief, but it will be possible for us to bring greater understanding to bear on life from this point of view.[2]

Those who remain incarnated on the earth *can* add, transform, and work upon this relationship. They can add meaning, offer thoughts of spiritual understanding, may try to help the others who might not have had the time or inclination to learn about the land of the spirit in which they now find themselves. Those who remain behind can, in all their suffering, help to shed some light of orientation for the ones who may wander in relative sleep and darkness in a world they cannot experience, because they did not learn to know it.

Rudolf Steiner describes how it is that the sensory world, in which we live, waits for us to learn about it, to differentiate and to perceive it step by step, and add to the concepts that enrich our sense perceptions. In the other, spiritual, world, it is different; only those areas are lit up for us for which we have acquired the understanding. We recognize only what we have begun to know here on earth.

Therefore, our effort to try to form images and ideas that transcend all physical sensory dimensions—that try to follow our beloved friend into other realms of existence—will not only be like Orpheus trying desperately to find and recall his Eurydice, but it can transcend our need to know, and, in the acceptance of God's will and the spiritual laws that guide all our destinies, we can try to accompany the way the other needs must go, and if possible attempt to lighten and warm it for him or her. We must no longer cling to *our* child as to a precious possession, but we can learn to think that the experience he or she has of him or herself is now quite different from what it had been here on earth. In earthly life we tend to know ourselves as we appear in our bodily form. When this body has been laid aside, how can we think of ourselves in a purely spiritual dimension? How can we learn to appreciate the meaning of the words, as given in the prayer: "And what appears to you through thinking / As your Self in the land of souls /May accept our love." Is this that Self, that inner Self, that had been there always, even when we identified ourselves with the body in which we lived before death?

What do we know of the "Self" that is the other's true Self? This leads to the next question, which is . . .

8

Who Are You?

The question, How can I understand the destiny that led you to your early death? arises powerfully. Strangely enough the question, Who are you? never seems to arise while the daily cares and the hustle and bustle of a child's life occupy the days. Maybe it should have arisen at the time of birth.

Where did you come from? What will your life be like? What were your aims before you came to earth?

Thank you for entrusting yourself to me, to my care, and thank you for your companionship. Here, too, the external arrangements, the cares for a small child's physical well-being, seem to preoccupy the mind. The whole process of pregnancy and birth is so totally beyond our comprehension. Life happens in us, and through us. We give part of ourselves to let a child grow; we form her body and give her birth. But what happens really? We hardly dare to begin to think about it. Never can one experience so tangibly, so closely, the working of God the Father, who created heaven, earth, and all the creatures that inhabit this planet, than during the time of pregnancy.

The only other equally strong moment of encounter with the Almighty God's power is when the child takes leave again. The beloved body lies in the coffin, lifeless, motionless, and no power on earth can make her stir, open her eyes, speak, not even a last word of farewell. This, too, is beyond our grasp; it is unfathomable. Our thoughts come to a standstill, and we sense the world of matter—the deep abyss known to all times between this and the spiritual world is described in different mythologies. Our own sense of reality is shaken in this encounter.

Who are you? Why did you leave? If we want to understand other people, we may do so best by looking at their biography. For example, events that colored their lives, the way they faced them, the way they led their lives, and how they changed their destinies. What *is* our destiny? It is intangible, and so often enacted by others coming toward us.

In the event of an unexpected, untimely, early death, be it through illness or through violence in any form, destiny had hardly a chance to begin to unfold. All hopes lie shattered, so it seems.

Did you really want to go so early? we ask. Was it your will, dear love? Is it best for you?

Others offer answers such as, "God's will is always best," or "She may have been spared a troublesome adolescence." These answers may have some truth in them, but they sound too functional, too partial and earthly when one is confronted with existential loss.

The question arises in one: "What does it mean for a child when it is torn out of life suddenly by an accident? What kind of child is it? Is there perhaps a spiritual gain that will bear fruit in a later life due to the forceful experience of death?

It seems a very different kind of child that suffers the destiny of dying from a long terminal illness. These children appear to me mostly incredibly wise and mature. Their suffering may well create a deep inner strength for a future life.

Death forces us to face the spiritual dimension of human beings as, for example, in the words of the Gospel of John: "The wind blows where it will; you hear the sound of it, but you do not know where it comes from or where it is going. So with everyone who is born from spirit."

I took refuge in much reading. I read and reread Rudolf Steiner's works. In the years 1914–1918, he spoke much about the question of life and death. He gave advice to the many who had lost their sons and fathers in World War I. The continued life of the spirits of men spoke through his words; it restored comfort.

Friends have often quoted to me from these lectures. Steiner says that the life forces of a person dying young have not been used up to sustain her life for its full sixty or seventy years, but have remained unused. They have been released—given back to the cosmos—and now can be used by higher angelic beings for the good of the world, a world that is in need of healing life-forces, for human beings work at its destruction.

Looked at from a wider point of view, an element of sacrifice is apparent. It requires much selfless concern for the world and humanity as a whole to accept that this sacrifice may have had to be brought by your only child. The soul, which grows in ultimate love, aches at the increasing pains inflicted on it, when it is asked to accept this point of view, however true it may be. It requires a kind of communion with all things, all becoming, which grows only very slowly.

It is good to read—again in Steiner—that it is precisely this very selfless, conscious communion with the world and its further becoming that *may* make it possible to encounter our friends on the other side of death. But it demands much overcoming. There is no cheating the all-seeing, all-aware, all-knowing spirit!

One has to try and include this perspective of sacrifice in one's search for the meaning of an early death.

Rudolf Steiner helps us further with what he tells

us—and I will quote him below verbatim, for he is very conscientious in describing only what he has confirmed, has proved, and has reconfirmed through his ability of spiritual perception. He leads us steadily to the consideration of reincarnation. If anything is to make sense and have meaning, and if we are not only to be specks of dust in a game of chance, reincarnation becomes the logical conclusion.

Most descriptions of life between death and a new birth deal with ordinary deaths, or people who have lived their lives to the appointed end. Thus, we search for any indication of understanding when there is a sudden death of a child on the road. There are very few references to this.

It was such a help to me when I found one, that I want to quote it here. It opened a new vista that combined the personal and individual tasks with the needs of the whole world.

It is necessary, if one wants to have an exact image of the first years or decades of life after death, that one compares how this life forms itself in the case of human beings who die young, say, who die in their first years of childhood, and how it is with those who die later, towards the middle of their lives, and then again, with those who die at a ripe old age. Things are highly differentiated. In reality, life after death is very different, depending on whether one has died early or late, and a true picture can only arise by comparing the experiences in people who have died at different ages of their lives.

Thus, it is, for instance, important in order to arrive at certain things, to convince oneself how it is with those who have left life at a very early stage, let us say as small children, and then again with those who left life at the age of eleven, twelve, and thirteen years of age. It is really a big difference that one can observe for the life after death, whether a man died before reaching his eighth or ninth year, or before his sixteenth or seventeenth year. This is clearly noticeable from certain experiences one can have with the dead. Thus, one can observe with people who died very early, in their tenderest childhood, that after death they are very, very engaged in tasks concerned with mankind during the time that follows directly after their death.[1]

Rudolf Steiner continues that lecture by saying that it is a fallacy to believe that an old man remains an old man after death, or that a small child remains a small child.

. . . Even if I would die as a child of only three to six months of age, all the many previous lives on earth come into consideration, and I can thus enter the spiritual world as a mature soul. It is totally wrong to imagine that a child continues to live as a child. One finds that souls of children who died early received tasks that belong closely with what the earth needs, as a spiritual wellspring, for its further development. I would say that men cannot work on earth without receiving impulses that come from spiritual spheres. They don't come in a wishy-washy way as general pantheism would want us to believe; they come from real beings, and among those we find the souls of children who died an early death . . .

If, however, children die who are nine to ten years of age, but not yet sixteen or seventeen years old, then one finds them quite soon after death in the company of spiritual beings. But those spiritual beings are human souls. One finds them in such company with human souls, and specifically with those who are waiting for their next incarnation. Those human beings who die in very early childhood are engaged with people down here. Those that died between the ages of seven or eight to sixteen or seventeen years one finds concerned with souls who are aiming to reincarnate very soon. This is then for these souls of considerable help and support, one could say, for these souls who die young are important messengers for what those awaiting reincarnation will need, in order to prepare themselves for a new earthly existence. It is vital to know this, if one does not want to indulge in generalities, but really wishes to penetrate into the spiritual worlds.[2]

He also says the following:

In considering the deeper meaning of the evolution of life, it would be particularly interesting to consider what it means when people die during different ages of life. Let us say, for example, we follow the soul of an eleven-, twelve-, or thirteen-year-old girl or boy, who has gone through the portal of death at that age.

In this case it holds good that the ether body retains unused forces, which theoretically would have been sufficient for all the years of life to follow.... It generally holds good that a man prepares himself for death throughout his whole life, because to some extent our whole life is such a preparation, insofar as we work towards the destruction of our life. If we were unable to destroy it, we would never be able to reach a degree of perfection, because we achieve this perfection only by the destruction of our physical body.

If a person goes through the portal of death at the age of thirteen, a long period of undoing or destruction that would otherwise have taken place, does not happen; he need not do what would have been done, and this manifests in a most peculiar way.

If we follow such a soul, we can find her after a relatively short time in, I would say, most remarkable companionship. We find her amidst souls who are engaged in preparing for a new life, and who are about to reincarnate quite soon. The souls of those who have gone through death in their eleventh, twelfth, and thirteenth year of life, are placed among these souls. And if one concerns oneself more specifically with these circumstances one sees, to one's astonishment, that the souls about to enter a new life on earth are in need of just what these other souls can bring up from the earth in order to gain the strength they need to incarnate.

Thus, the youthful souls provide powerful help to those souls who have to return to the earth in the immediate future.

Such help, which can be given under normal circumstances by young children who were quite ordinary and who had in no way a spiritually outstanding life, but who were simply lively, alert children, can no longer be given by those who die at a later age; the latter have another task. Everyone has to accept his karma and one must not think: I would like to die at this or that age; one dies when it is in accordance with one's karma. The help that one can give to souls awaiting their new incarnation cannot be given if one dies later . . .

If a child of one year who is still very close to the spiritual leaves the physical plane, it is very soon in the spiritual world. This is the case up to the fourteenth year; until then one is in one's physical body in such a way that allows one to reach easily into the world of those souls about to seek a reincarnation . . .[3]

Dear Saskia, my love, if this is so, what a terrible chaos, what a fearful situation has become your field of action now! No wonder it needed a strong, healthy, positive kind of child! Our mind staggers at the imagination of what this sphere of entry into incarnation and birth must be like in our time. The chaos and the destiny of souls looking for their destined parents, of the rejections through a multitude of abortions, and so forth.

The fear and withdrawal of souls at the sight of what lies ahead!.

Rudolf Steiner explains that before birth each child sees his future life; his whole destiny lies in front of him like an open book. This can be a frightening experience in our time and civilization, which has become so hard, materialistic, and so filled with disaster; our world has little room for the unfolding of a soul-spirit in childhood.

How much courage does it need to take the plunge? How much support, reassurance, and positive love are needed to help these souls who are ready to be born in the immediate future? How much Michaelic courage, to be willing to enter the incarnation in the *Imitatio Christi* on earth? Entrusting one's life to the care of others . . . helplessly at the start.

Oh, dear love, my Saskia, how can I help you now? How can I help? How can I be a friend to you who has gone ahead into such enormous tasks? How can I send you thoughts that will ever strengthen you; ideas that will illuminate the meaning of the earth and human existence on this planet? How can I show you that the aim is that, in the distant future, the earth will be permeated by the forces of Christ, and that its ultimate purpose is to become a star, radiating love?

It often helps to turn to the Gospel of John, and sometimes to the lectures by Rudolf Steiner about it. They give help towards a deeper understanding of life on earth.

And then there is the prospect of seeing one another again, as one day we will be called to pass through the same gate at our own death. Time has different dimensions in that other world. It will not be long—you will meet again. This is comforting.

Others will remark wisely, "But of course, such a

young soul may spend but a brief time in the spiritual realm before incarnating again, having been strengthened for a new life." To start with, one does not want to hear such things! They take away the last hope for a reunion soon! These are the last traces of possessiveness. No one *belongs* to us ! It is all a question of *free giving*. Individual yet mutual growth is helped by communion between us.

Allow the other to grow and go her way. Pray to the angel that guides her eternal path, and, who knows, one day in some mysterious way, you may be collaborators or friends in a greater task, having gained in strength through all the suffering for each other. As Max Reuschle expressed it:

But the Radiant Ones
Go early back to God
To prepare in the depth
Their living return.

9

For All Children with Open Hearts: The Child Who Heard the Angels Weep

At night we go to sleep because we need rest. Clever people tell us that we need this rest; our legs are tired, our arms ache and our eyes are closing. Some say our muscles are fatigued, or our nerves are overstrained. Are they right?

Yes and no. Of course our legs get tired, and so do our arms and our eyes. But I don't feel sleepy because of my legs, but because of myself. It is my spirit, or my soul, that wants to rest. Why? Because the soul feels lonely after a day on earth and longs for heaven. The soul longs to be with the guardian angel in order to remember again what it has come to earth for. That is the real reason why we go to sleep. Leaving our body behind, our soul soars to the palace of heaven in order to be received by our angel.

The guardian angel leads the soul into the palace of heaven, and there in the first room we meet a big angel, who is spinning all the time. There are windows on either side of the room. After we have greeted the big angel, we go with our guardian angel to look through the windows on one side. Through these windows we can observe the past day, and look upon what we have done, both good and bad. Then we go to the other side and when we look out, we see what is waiting for us on the following day, and how we should best accomplish what we must do.

Then we are led around in the palace of heaven. Some

doors are open; others remain closed—just as is good and necessary for the soul. Even if we realize that what we have done during the day was not right and even harmful, this night experience in the palace of heaven is mainly a happy experience. If we are not too sleepy during the day, in our mind we see what we can do to make up for our misbehaving; we know that our angel will help us. But we do not only see our own deeds, but also those of other souls. As a result, we may decide to help others here and there. Yet one can say that each soul is led its own way, according to what is necessary and possible. Now there was once a child whose soul went up to the palace of heaven at night. After he had looked back at the previous day with his angel, he was led into the palace. While they were walking around, the child suddenly stopped.

"Listen!" the child said. They could hear without doubt that somebody was crying, softy and quietly. The sound was so sad that it made the child's heart sore.

"Who is crying?" the child asked the angel. The angel only shook his head and indicated that they should go on.

During the following day, the child could not recall what had happened the night before. But when that child entered the palace of heaven again that night, greeted the angel who was spinning, and looked through the windows, the memory came back to him. As they walked deeper into the palace of heaven, the child again heard the sobbing.

"Listen!" the child said again to the angel. They stood quietly, and in this silence, they could hear once more that someone was crying, softly and meekly, and yet so sadly that it pained the child's heart.

"Who is crying?" the child asked the angel. Again the angel shook his head and indicated that they should walk on. The child, however, noticed a little difference, for happiness shone out of the angel's eyes.

Again the child could not remember during the following day what he had experienced the previous night; he simply felt that he was waiting for something, but what it was he did not know. Thus, the third night came, and everything happened as in the nights before. When the child had passed the angel who was spinning and was walking through the palace of heaven together with his angel, he suddenly heard the weeping again.

"Listen!" he said as he stopped walking. While he was listening, the child noticed that the angel had turned round to him, and that his face shone with joy. The child saw the angel's shining face; he was amazed, and he repeated his question. "Who is weeping?"

This time the angel answered, "I can show you, if you wish. But if you see it, you can never again be the same happy child you are now."

"I cannot be happy anyway," replied the child, "for my heart aches and pains every night. Please, lead me on."

So they followed the sound of the weeping until they came to a room that was closed off by a dark veil. There the angel said, "I cannot lead you further. If you wish to see those who are weeping, you must lift the veil yourself and enter unguided."

For a moment the child hesitated. Should he go on? His heart urged him to proceed. He lifted the veil and entered the room; the child's guardian angel now followed him.

The child could hardly believe his eyes. He looked around for a long time. He could hardly believe what he saw was actually true. The room was filled with angels. They wept so softly and so quietly. This was all the more agonizing.

At last the child took a deep breath and spoke to one of the weeping angels. "I never knew that angels could weep. Heaven is such a happy place! Please, tell me why you are weeping?"

The angel answered, "We weep because we have lost human beings. We cannot reach them any longer, and so our hands are bound."

"And why is that so?" the child asked.

The angel gazed upon the child for a while before he answered. The child noticed that he was weeping less than before. "It is because they have no love," said the angel. "Only love can bind beings together. Everyone who wants to enter the palace of heaven must bring at least a little bit of love for his angel. If there is no love at all, we cannot lead him."

And then he told the child, "I am the angel of a rich merchant, whose ships sail all the oceans of the earth, and bring him wealth in great abundance. His soul was that of an explorer when I led him down to earth to be born. He wished to know and unite all peoples. But since money has flowed into his pocket, his love has vanished, and only greed is left. He could do such a lot with his wealth; however, he does not know it because I cannot reach him." And, pointing around, the angel ended, "This is what all of us experience."

"And is there no help?" asked the child quietly.

The effect of this question was quite amazing. All of a sudden the weeping stopped, the angels looked up, and here and there the child noticed the glimmer of a smile.

The angel looked at the child for a time, as if to examine him, before he replied, "Yes, there is. If someone would sacrifice his love we would be helped."

"Is it that easy?" The question had escaped from his

lips before the child had even thought of speaking. If it was simply a matter of giving love, he could give them some more. The gaze of the angel, though, told the child that something more difficult was involved. And he realized this when the angel said, "To sacrifice to us the love that enables us to help is not at all easy for a child of the earth, because you must not give us any of the love with which you love other beings, your parents, your brothers, sisters, the animals, or the plants of the earth. Only the love with which you love your life, can you sacrifice."

The child looked at the angel, and his whole face was one big question. What was he talking about? The angel explained. "You see, it is love that allows you to live on earth. You like to walk around, play, look around, behold things, speak, and sing. The love for these things, for these abilities in yourself, this love alone can you sacrifice. And only children can do so, grownups can no longer set this love free. That is why it is so difficult to find help."

The child now believed the seriousness of the angel's words. He had to struggle to speak the next words. Although he spoke very quietly, all the angels understood what he said.

"If I offer the love I have for my life," asked the child, "will that then be enough?"

He was no longer amazed to see the angel shaking his head again. He had by now understood very well that the problem was not so easy.

"There are many children who would be willing to do that," replied the angel, "but one more thing is necessary, and that is that you have good friends on earth, who really love you. They must help you fulfill your tasks, the old ones and the new ones. Do you remember your old tasks?"

"Yes," nodded the child. "I was going to be a carpenter."

"To help people and make their surroundings beautiful," agreed the angel. "And therefore, you would then need the hands of your friends."

"Would they understand me?"

"If they love you, they will understand you."

Then the child felt the hand of the guardian angel on his shoulder. "Let us go now. Think about it, before you say yes or no."

The next day the child was wide awake. He was not conscious of the experiences of the previous night, but he was conscious of his surroundings, helping where he could, and trying to be as friendly as possible. He enjoyed the day very much because the people were also friendly to him.

That night, after passing through the room with the spinning angel, the child met the weeping angels a second time, and said to them, "I have many friends who love me. But will they be able to keep on loving me even if I cannot jump around any longer, or see, or sing?"

"If they are real friends, they will be able to keep on loving you," was the reply, "and we might be able to help them a little."

The following day the child felt like playing with two particular friends. They had a wonderful time. The child was hardly surprised when he met the two others in the palace of heaven that night as he entered the veiled room. Each of the children had a bright cross shining on his forehead.

"Are you ready?" asked the angel.

"We are," replied the children in unison.

"And is there one among you who would have the patience to sacrifice his love and still remain on earth for three days in order to help your friends find you more quickly and in order to understand you?" the angel went on to ask. "You will have to stay there without being able to walk, to see, or to sing."

"I would be willing to do that," answered the children in one voice.

The angel smiled at them. "Then it shall be you," said he, pointing to one of the children. "And we shall all be around you, keeping you company." Then he indicated to the children that they should follow him. He led them to another room, that at first did not look special at all.

"Here," the angel explained, "you can see and find yourselves united with whoever you want to be united with."

The children looked around, but saw nothing. Then the angel said, "You must think of someone or something. Just try it."

So they thought of home. Almost immediately they saw their houses and families—everyone was fast asleep. Then they thought of their school, and it appeared. Finally they remembered their good friends, and they became visible.

"Can we talk to them?" the children asked.

"You can," replied the angel, "but they would probably not understand yet."

When the children entered the palace of heaven again they looked a bit sad. This time they all came together. They greeted the big angel who was spinning, and went to look through the windows that revealed the previous day. Then they walked to the other windows to look at the future day, but they could not see anything.

When they turned around, the big angel had stopped spinning. He held three balls of finely spun thread in his hands. Each child received one of them. They also

71

saw that a golden thread was spun into each of the balls.

Then they walked into the palace of heaven and to the veiled room where they had met the weeping angels. They said to the angels, "We bring you the sacrifice of our love for our lives. May it help you and those poor loveless people on earth."

There was weeping no longer. The faces of the angels became radiant, their eyes sparkled; there was utter joy among them. This comforted the children.

"Come now," said the angel, "and let us see what is happening on earth."

So together they went to the room that they had seen for the first time the previous night. They all thought of a similar incident and all of a sudden they could see that one of them was not as free as the others. A string of light was fettered to a body that lay on a bed without moving; the eyes and mouth were closed.

The parents of the child were standing at the bedside. Deep sorrow spoke out of their eyes. "I am here, Mother," called the child, "I am here, Father!" But the parents did not look up. Then the child tried to stroke them, but they could not feel it.

"Oh angel," said the child then, "I think I must go back! They do not hear, they do not feel. Let me not lose them!"

"You have not lost them," replied the angel. "Give them another day to find you."

The child was pleased that the other two children were there, too; that made it easier to have patience.

Thus the second day came, and the child called, "I am here, Mother; I am here, Father!" But the parents did not look up.

The child stroked them, and all of a sudden the mother said, "I don't know, but I have the feeling that our dear child is not sick. Do you think that he can see us?"

And the father nodded his head. "I think so, yes. I think so."

"Did they feel the stroking?" asked the child.

"They felt it in their hearts," said the angel. "Soon they will understand you."

The child looked down at the parents again and thought, If only they would stop crying for me. If only they knew that I am all right.

Then the mother looked up and said, "Let's not weep. Our child is probably well and our weeping can only make him sad, too."

The child heard it. "They understood," he cried. "Oh, they understood!" But he asked the angel, "How could they understand, when I was only just thinking?"

The angel smiled. "Because they love you. Did you not know that your heart understands the thoughts of someone you love?"

When the third day came, the child called once more, "I am here, Mother. I am here, Father."

The parents did not look up, but the father said thoughtfully, "Our child is not sick, but more healthy than the two of us. One day we shall find him again."

And when the child stroked his mother, she replied, "I feel him already now. My heart is not sore any longer. Our child must be very close to us."

When the child heard that, he jubilated. "They hear and they understand!"

"And they will hear and understand better still as time goes by. Come now," called the angel. Then the child came towards him, and the string of light vanished.

The children stayed in the palace of heaven; they were united with everyone in their thoughts. There were some people who did not understand them, but there were others who did, for their love for the children had opened their hearts.

There was something else that the children who had sacrificed their love for life could do: Every night, when the souls of their friends soared to the palace of heaven, they met and talked to them; some of their friends even remembered some of the conversation when they awoke the next morning.

Did the soul of the rich merchant find its way again to the palace of heaven? I am almost certain that he did—he and many others. Tonight I shall ask my friends about it, and I hope that I shall not forget the answer. And that is how it happened. Yes, that is how it is . . .[1]

10

Reincarnation

As the story in this book entails a serious consideration of reincarnation of individuals, it may be good to add some aspects of reincarnation at this point. The wish for continuation of some sort of existence beyond death is, consciously or subconsciously, surely present in all human beings. It is possibly an understandable, if egoistic, wish to survive death at the end of life. For thousands of years prior to our time the idea of reincarnation and karma has been part of the concept of life. Perhaps it could be called wishful thinking by those who do not want to or cannot find a reality in such a thought. Maybe a better question—because it is much freer from personal selfishness—would be, "Where did each of us come from?" Or, "Where were our children when we were youngsters?" "In heaven" is the usual, somewhat unscientific answer. But how is this possible?

It depends, one can say, on how we individually experience ourselves. Are we only a body with some sensory-soul faculties. When we say, "I" to ourselves, what is this "I" in us? This so intimate, unique self-reflection happens perhaps too rarely, perhaps only under some form of stress or, of course, when consciously sought for.

A beautiful description of the nature of the "I" can be found in the essay by Jacques Lusseyran, entitled "Against The Pollution of the 'I'":

I told you that the *I* is fragile. It is not even something that we really own, a collection of faculties to which we could point with pride. It is a kind of vitality—yes, at most a kind of vitality. It is a force not far removed from its birth. It is a promise, if you will, given to man, that one day he will be as the universe, that one day he will see the world with eyes opened wide, that he will perceive himself and be able to recognize that there exists an ordered relationship, a necessary reciprocity between that world and himself. The *I*, in brief, is still so little that a mere nothing, as it were, suffices to rob us of it. And now I see it beleaguered and warred against!

Let us speak of the *I*, the true *I*. At least, let us try. What I call the *I* is that animation, that impulse, that allows me to make use of the four elements, of this earth on which I live, also of my intelligence and of my emotions—yes, even of my dreams. It is, in sum, a force that imbues me with a power afforded by no other force on earth: the power to live without waiting for life to come to me. The ego needs things, the greatest possible number of things—be they money, fame, approbation, power, reward. The *I* makes no such demands. When it is present, when it is at work, it sets its own world up against the other world, the world of things. The *I* is wealth in the midst of poverty. It is vital interest when all around are bored. It is hope, when all rational basis for hope is gone. From out of the *I* springs man's whole world of invention. And, finally, it is what we still have left when all else has been taken from us, when nothing comes to us from outside and yet our forces are sufficient to overcome the void.[1]

This "I," this central, inner reality of each human being, finds itself in varying life circumstances, in an inherited body, and in a geographical and cultural time environment. It works in these and creates new connections, new destinies, additional experiences and additional faculties.

Gotthold E. Lessing (1729–1781) puts it so poignantly in his essay, "The Education of the Human Species":

But why could not each individual human being have been more than once in this world? Is this hypothesis so ridiculous, because it is the oldest? Because human understanding has first come to it, before the sophistry of our schools has destroyed and weakened it? Why should I not return as often as I am able to receive new knowledge and new skills? Do I achieve so much in one go, that it is not worth the effort to return again?

Not because of this? Or should I not return because I have forgotten that I have already been here on earth before? Good for me that I have forgotten it. The memory of my previous conditions would only allow me to misuse my present situation. But have I forgotten it for now, must I therefore have forgotten it forever?

Or should I not return because I lose too much time with it? Lost time? But what have I to lose? Is Not All Eternity Mine?[2]

If we consider such thoughts, our life and the encounters with fellow human beings become so much deeper and richer in meaning. Although the reality of reincarnation has been known for thousands of years, in the Eastern philosophies and religions particularly, it is imbued with an added quality, as is all life after the beginning of our era, that is, after the birth of Christ. One can consider that each child that is born has decided to do so before he descended into the hereditary sheaths of father and mother.

If Christianity is such a decisive factor in world and

earth evolution, and one can learn to appreciate it, then one can learn from the Gospels that Christ promised to remain united with the earth and human evolution "to the end of the world."

We all, then, have a part in this evolution, in the fulfillment of the mission of the earth, together with Christ. Each child that is born—so we can learn from the spiritual insight of Rudolf Steiner—comes to the earth with a deep, primary intuition to experience, grow, learn, and work on the earth with its people. Each child hopes to join forces with the Christ in order to help transform the earth and its peoples. Each child's incarnation can be seen as a very personal *Imitatio Christi*—even though we all tend to forget this as we grow up.

During the trying times of individual adolescence—in the midst of all the inner turmoil—it might be a helpful aspect to consider the often buried, unperceived longing to know and to be assured again of the real task one sets out to meet, the zeal that makes life worthwhile. More often than not, such a desperate cry, possibly disguised by a lot of awkward nonconformity, is not being heard. The purely material terms of finding a career and earning one's living are all that is addressed. Then the individual "I" is often stunted and his wings are clipped for many years, if not decades, and that "I" needs to be rediscovered, often much later and often with much trouble, hardship, and despair.

Christianity does not strive to free itself from the need to be born again on earth. (This is the aim of many Eastern, Buddhist religions.) On the contrary, Christianity accepts that, if an individual believes in a deep, ultimate belonging together with his fellow beings and the earth, salvation can come. In the spirit of St. Paul: Mankind, with its various parts, is in its totality the

Body of Christ. We begin to understand our task as Christians when we accept each person as an essential part of that final redemption, transformation, and evolution of the earth and its people.

A superhuman amount of love is needed; love for *every* other fellow human being, because we begin to realize that we are all interdependent. The earth can only reach its spiritual goal, and with it humanity's fulfillment in connection with Christ, when every individual, yes, *every* individual, may he or she be ever so severely entangled in deep problems, has reached his or her true humanity. This is the overwhelming task inherent in Christianity. In one life we can only achieve parts of our destiny. So much needs to be made good; so much in the past is left unfinished; so much has caused injury to other people. We come to earth again and again—no matter how hard the conditions we may find upon entry—because we possess an ardent wish to make things right in our own karma. Also, we have a deep concern for humanity, the earth, and for a relationship with Christ. These add to our decision to reincarnate and do our bit.

Epilogue

This account of my personal path was written three years after the loss of my child, Saskia. It could only have been written then—or never, at least not in the very intimate, inward way in which you can partake.

Seven years have now passed. It belongs to the truth of our lives that although the empty space remains, the intensity of the pain of the soul gradually heals as a wound would in the body. This is especially true if we have tried to work it through, face it as consciously as possible without diversion of the mind, or escaping into outer activity.

What is the situation after seven years? It is perhaps unbelievable, but yet it is true as the old words say: Time heals all wounds. This is grace. However, with it goes the experience almost of a second loss. It can be described thus: during the intense grief of the first years the soul is lit up by pain. The "curtain" to the soul-spirit world is, as it were, torn open. Slowly, steadily, it closes again. The sensory world with its great strength again covers up the much gentler, much more subtle experiences of the soul, like the grass that grows over the patch of earth that was cut open to make the grave.

It is essential to try to have a clear consciousness, and give as much as possible of good thoughts and loving assistance to your child during the first years after her death. Later, one feels that the soul and spirit of the dead child seem to be further away—distant as it were —and on her way. She is not out of reach. No, not that. As often in life, one understands a situation better when

81

looking back on it later. You can know, just because time has moved on, and life has brought changes, that your child was very, very close to you during the first weeks and months after the death occurred. For me, some of the tangible proofs of this were my strong dreams, mentioned earlier, which ceased after the first year. It was your despair and pain that obscured your awareness and your perception then. And Christ was closer around you, too.

This last sentence may sound like a phrase, an expression of faith. Only now, so many years later and in the spirit of this book can I share my probably deepest experience connected with Saskia's death.

One day, in fact, exactly one month after the accident, I had a particularly desperate day. I was almost paralyzed with intense pain, which reached into the physical, over a particular thing I felt I had omitted to do for Saskia. That night I had no dreams; it was only total darkness. However, on waking up early next morning, I saw Saskia briefly; my main experience was of an indescribable golden light that was at the same time intense warmth and love and peace; it permeated and surrounded my soul.

At the time I attributed all this to Saskia, but later on I understood that I had in fact inwardly reached such an intense level of despair that this was like an experience of reaching the threshold myself. I will never forget the warmth, love, and golden lightness that permeated me, so unlike any sense experience. Was this the light, the warmth, the loving strength and peace of Christ?

Maybe this book can help those who are in the midst of the immediacy of the experience of death to be more open and sensitive. However, in no situation would it be right to say that the death of my child is too long ago; I have missed it. It is never too late to awaken to your child's presence around you, even though it may have become much more subtle and less clearly perceptible.

But life does go on, even when we would wish it to stand still and to stop . . . and the footprints of a precious life threaten to be blown over and disappear.

A very special friend of mine, who also helped to work over this manuscript initially and supported me in bringing these descriptions into print, Anke Weihs, wrote a very fine letter to me. She describes beautifully what I would like to put at the end of this little book.

It occurred to me that as a soul continues to expand in the infinite world, and its connection to the earth, and to those human beings left behind grows more spiritualized, one can experience a kind of *second loss*—and with a child that expansion happens more quickly than with an older person. One's own experience of "possessiveness" in the best sense towards that soul becomes strained and is, indeed, no longer adequate, for want of a better word.

I recently came across a booklet by C. S. Lewis called *The Four Loves*. The first love he calls "need-love"—one loves because one needs love. It is a deep and profound mutuality between mother and child, person and person, person and God. Out of need-love springs one's grief, one's longing, one's search.

But then Lewis speaks of "gift-love," that love that contains no need, no mutuality, no return. It is simply a free gift. To me it is as though I would make my heart into a bowl of incense, the smoke of which rises up in offering to the being I love and vanishes into the air, the clouds. In gift-love, if one imagines it like this, there is no possessiveness, no grief; there is only faithfulness, day and night.

I don't think that one can oneself so easily overcome need-love; the wound of severance scars over, but the scar remains. But I think that in the spiritual nature of things, need-love transforms *itself*. Archbishop Runcie here in Britain, an intelligent and sensitive man, says in connection with mourning and the gradual change away from mourning that one must learn to "manage one's memories," and not let them manage us. Then grieving and the flattening out of grieving become creative and ongoing. Thus is the experience of a "second loss," a loss of one's acute grief, transformed and nothing and no one can prevent one from lighting one's bowl of incense, one's offering of gift-love.[1]

And thus, we live on.

Notes

Chapter 1, The First Days

[1]Matthew 28:2-6.

[2]Mabel Collins, *Light on the Path* (San Francisco: Theosophical University Press, 1976).

Chapter 2, The Search

[1]Raymond A. Moody, *Life after Life* (New York: Bantam, 1975).

[2]Helen Greave, *Testimony of Light* (London: World Fellowship Press, 1969).

[3]George Ritchie, *Return from Tomorrow* (Eastbourne, U.K.: Kingsway Publications, 1980).

[4]Stanley Drake, *Though You Die* (Eastbourne, U.K.: Christian Community Press, 1962).

[5]Rudolf Steiner, *Unsere Toten (Our Dead)* (Dornach, Switzerland: Rudolf Steiner Nachlassverwaltung, 1962). Not translated.

[6]Rudolf Steiner, *The Dead Are With Us* (London: Rudolf Steiner Press, 1985). See also: *Living Links between the Living and the Dead* (London: Rudolf Steiner Press, 1973).

Chapter 3, Help We Can Give

[1]Rudolf Steiner, "Exact Spiritual Knowledge of Supersensible Worlds," lecture, November 17, 1922. Not translated.

[2]Rudolf Steiner, *Theosophy* (Hudson, N.Y.: Anthroposophic Press, 1986).

[3]These parables can be found in the Gospel of Matthew.

[4]Maria Reimann, *Licht vom unerschopften Lichte* (Stuttgart: Urachhaus, 1983).

Chapter 7, Can You Feel Her?

[1]Rudolf Steiner, "Karmische Wirkungen," lecture, October 24, 1916. Not translated.
[2]Ibid.

Chapter 8, Who Are You?

[1]Rudolf Steiner, *The Occult Movement in the Nineteenth Century and its Relationship to the Culture of the World* (London: Rudolf Steiner Press, 1973).
[2]Rudolf Steiner, "Schicksalsbildung und das Leben nach dem Tode," lecture, November 16, 1915. Not translated.

Chapter 9, For All Children with Open Hearts: The Child Who Heard the Angels Weep

[1]This story was told to a group of handicapped children by Reverend Georg Dreissig, priest of the Christian Community Church.

Chapter 10, Reincarnation

[1]Jacques Lusseyran, *Against the Pollution of the "I"* Myrin Institute Proceedings No. 30 (New York: Myrin Institute, 1975), pp. 12-13.
[2]Gotthold Ephraim Lessing, *Education of Mankind*, 1780.

Epilogue

[1]**C. S. Lewis,***The Four Loves* (New York: Harcourt Brace, 1971).

About the Author

Karin von Schilling was born in 1933 in Saskatchewan, Canada. Her parents, both academically qualified, had emigrated there after losing their estates in Estonia during the Russian Revolution. She spent her first four years in a homestead on the open prairies of Canada.

Her parents returned to Germany in 1937. World War II broke out, and Karin spent her childhood in many different places due to the threat of warfare. In 1945, she returned to Berlin, her parents' home; she experienced the Russian invasion, and the airlift in the largely ruined city. Yet, in the outer devastation of that time, there was much spiritual endeavor and activity; she searched for a deeper meaning of life.

These experiences prompted Karin to search for spiritual social values and spiritual tasks. At the age of eighteen, she travelled to Scotland in order to begin curative educational training for work with handicapped children, in the Camphill (Rudolf Steiner) Schools outside Aberdeen. Karin worked for twenty years in close proximity with children suffering from multiple handicaps: blindness, deafness, paralysis, retardation and epilepsy. As her main task, she worked for fifteen years as a class teacher; she also spent some years in England and Ireland as a teachers' adviser.

Answering a call of real need, Karin decided to move to South Africa in 1971 with her daughter Saskia. Here she endeavored, together with a few others, to re-establish a Camphill Center, Cresset House, between Johannesburg and Pretoria. Cresset House became a residential training center for about sixty small children and adolescents in need of special care.

An essential aspect of Karin's work was to create a community base and to train young coworkers. The objective was to achieve a responsible relationship with their work, the children, and, in the process, with themselves. This she found wonderful and worthwhile, but at times also a strenuous task.

Karin von Schilling is an active member of the Anthroposophical Society as well as the Christian Community. At the time of writing this manuscript, she is principal of Cresset House.